HOW TO CREATE CPN NUMBERS FOR BEGINNERS

A Step by Step guide on how to create CPN numbers and lawfully improve your credit score

Table of Contents

INTRODUCTION 3
CHAPTER 1 11
   What is CPN numbers and their purpose .11
   Difference between CPNs and SSNs........14
CHAPTER 2 23
   Credit report and how CPNs fit into the credit system...23
   How CPNs can be used to build or repair credit..30
CHAPTER 3 39
   Step-by-step guide on how to legally obtain a CPN 39
CHAPTER 4 49
Tips for choosing a reputable CPN provider or service 49

INTRODUCTION

Hello there, If you're here, you've likely heard about CPN numbers and their potential to transform your financial landscape. Perhaps you're looking to repair damaged credit, safeguard your personal information, or simply explore alternative avenues for financial security. For whatever reason, you've arrived at the ideal location.

I have walked the path you're about to embark on. Like many, I found myself facing financial challenges and grappling with the limitations of traditional credit systems. Frustrated by the barriers in my way, I delved into the world of CPN numbers, seeking a solution that would empower me to take control of my financial future.

Through trial and error, extensive research, and consultations with experts, I uncovered the secrets to effectively leveraging CPNs to my advantage. I've seen firsthand the transformative impact that a well-managed CPN can have on one's creditworthiness and overall financial well-being.

But my journey wasn't without its obstacles. Along the way, I encountered misinformation, scams, and legal pitfalls that threatened to derail my progress. It was through these challenges that I gained invaluable insights and wisdom, which I'm eager to share with you in this book.

This book is a comprehensive roadmap crafted from real-life experience. Whether you're a complete novice or someone familiar with the concept of CPNs, this book will equip you with the knowledge and tools needed to navigate the complexities of CPN creation and usage with confidence.

What sets this book apart is its emphasis on legality, ethics, and responsible financial management. Unlike some resources that may promote dubious practices or skirt around legal boundaries, this book prioritizes compliance and transparency. I firmly believe that the key to long-term success lies in building a solid foundation of integrity and accountability.

Throughout these pages, you'll find practical advice, actionable strategies, and insider tips gleaned from years of hands-on experience. Whether you're seeking to build credit, protect your identity, or explore alternative financial avenues, you'll find everything you need to know within these chapters.

So, if you're ready to embark on a journey of financial empowerment, I invite you to dive deep into this and discover the possibilities that await. Together, we'll unlock the secrets to leveraging CPNs to their fullest potential and chart a course toward a brighter financial future.

CHAPTER 1

What is CPN numbers and their purpose

CPN, or Credit Privacy Number, is a nine-digit identification number that some individuals use as an alternative to their Social Security Number (SSN) when applying for credit. CPNs are sometimes marketed as a way to protect one's SSN from identity theft or to rebuild credit.

The primary purpose of a CPN is to provide a level of privacy and security for individuals concerned about sharing their SSN for various financial transactions. By using a CPN instead of an SSN, individuals aim to shield their sensitive personal information from potential identity thieves or unauthorized access.

However, it's crucial to understand that CPNs are not issued or recognized by the government, nor do they replace an SSN for legal or tax purposes. CPNs do not confer any special privileges or rights, and their use is subject to legal and regulatory scrutiny.

While CPNs may be marketed as a tool for improving credit or starting fresh financially, it's essential to approach their use with caution. Some tactics associated with CPNs may involve fraudulent or illegal activities, such as misrepresenting one's identity or engaging in credit repair schemes.

Difference between CPNs and SSNs

Imagine you're sitting at your kitchen table, staring at a stack of bills and credit card statements, feeling overwhelmed and frustrated. You've been struggling to make ends meet, and your credit score seems stuck in a downward spiral. You know you need to take action, but the idea of sharing your Social Security Number (SSN) for yet another credit application makes you uneasy. That's where CPN numbers come into play.

I remember that feeling all too well. Like many others, I found myself in a financial bind, grappling with the limitations of traditional credit systems. I knew I needed to rebuild my credit, but I was hesitant to expose my SSN to potential risks of identity theft or misuse.

That's when I first heard about CPN numbers—a seemingly magical solution that promised privacy and security in the world of credit. But before diving in headfirst, I needed to understand the fundamental differences between CPNs and SSNs. Let's start with the basics: your Social Security Number, that nine-digit identifier issued by the government, is the cornerstone of your financial identity. It's tied to everything from your taxes and employment records to your credit history and benefits eligibility. Your SSN is as personal as it gets, and safeguarding it is paramount to protecting your identity and financial well-being.

On the other hand, a CPN, or Credit Privacy Number, is a non-governmental identification number that some individuals use as an alternative to their SSN for certain financial transactions. Unlike an SSN, which is universally recognized and regulated, CPNs operate in a gray area of the credit landscape.

One key difference between CPNs and SSNs lies in their origins and legitimacy. Your SSN is issued by the Social Security Administration, a federal agency tasked with administering social insurance programs. It's backed by laws and regulations governing its use and protection. In contrast, CPNs are not issued or recognized by any government entity. They're often marketed as a way to shield your SSN from potential risks, such as identity theft or fraud, by providing a separate identifier for credit-related activities.

However, this distinction comes with important caveats. While using a CPN may offer a layer of privacy and security, it's essential to understand that CPNs do not replace your SSN for legal or tax purposes. They're not a shortcut to financial freedom or a get-out-of-debt card. In fact, some tactics associated with CPNs may skirt the boundaries of legality and morality, potentially exposing you to legal repercussions or financial harm.

In my journey with CPNs, I learned that transparency and responsibility are key. While it's tempting to seek quick fixes or shortcuts to financial success, the reality is that building good credit takes time, effort, and discipline. Using a CPN responsibly means understanding its limitations and risks, as well as adhering to the laws and regulations governing credit and identity.

CHAPTER 2

Credit report and how CPNs fit into the credit system

Credit reporting is like a digital fingerprint of your financial life, documenting your borrowing and repayment habits for lenders to assess your creditworthiness. Every time you open a credit card, take out a loan, or make a payment, that information gets recorded by credit bureaus—companies like Experian, Equifax, and TransUnion—that compile it into a comprehensive report.

Your credit report serves as a roadmap of your financial journey, detailing your accounts, balances, payment history, and more. It's a snapshot of your reliability as a borrower, helping lenders predict the likelihood that you'll repay your debts on time. And at the heart of it all is your credit score, a numerical representation of your creditworthiness based on the information in your report.

Now, where do CPN numbers come into play? Well, think of CPNs as a parallel universe within the credit system—a separate identifier that some individuals use to shield their Social Security Numbers (SSNs) from certain financial transactions. When you apply for credit using a CPN instead of your SSN, your activity gets linked to that alternate identifier, creating a distinct credit profile.

At first glance, this might seem like a game-changer—a way to build credit or repair a tarnished score without exposing your SSN to potential risks. But here's where things get complicated: while CPNs offer a level of privacy and security, they're not universally recognized or regulated like SSNs.

Credit bureaus and lenders rely on your SSN as a primary means of verifying your identity and assessing your creditworthiness. When you use a CPN, you're essentially operating in a gray area of the credit landscape, where the rules are murky and the consequences can be severe.

In my experience, navigating this gray area requires caution and diligence. While CPNs may offer a measure of privacy, they also come with risks—both legal and financial. Using a CPN responsibly means understanding its limitations and potential implications, as well as staying informed about changes in regulations and practices.

Ultimately, your credit report is a reflection of your financial behavior, regardless of whether you use an SSN or a CPN. Building and maintaining good credit requires responsible borrowing, timely payments, and a commitment to financial health. While CPNs may offer a degree of privacy, they're not a shortcut to financial success. So, as you explore the world of CPN numbers, remember to tread carefully, do your research, and seek guidance from trusted sources. After all, your financial future is too important to leave to chance.

How CPNs can be used to build or repair credit

Using a CPN to build or repair credit is like having a secret weapon in your arsenal—a tool that allows you to navigate the credit landscape with a level of privacy and security that traditional methods may not offer. But like any tool, it's essential to understand how to wield it effectively and responsibly.

So, how exactly can CPNs be used to build or repair credit? Let's break it down:

Establishing New Credit Lines: One of the most common strategies for using a CPN to build credit is to open new credit accounts. Whether it's a secured credit card, a retail store card, or a small personal loan, having a CPN allows you to apply for credit without relying on your Social Security Number (SSN). By making timely payments and keeping balances low, you can demonstrate responsible borrowing behaviour and gradually improve your credit score.

Diversifying Your Credit Portfolio: Credit scoring models take into account the types of accounts you have, known as your credit mix. By using a CPN to open different types of credit accounts, such as instalment loans or revolving lines of credit, you can diversify your credit portfolio and potentially boost your credit score. This shows lenders that you can responsibly manage various types of credit, which can work in your favour when applying for future loans or credit cards.

Repairing Damaged Credit: If you've experienced financial setbacks that have negatively impacted your credit, such as late payments, collections, or bankruptcies, using a CPN to start fresh can be an appealing option. By establishing new credit accounts with your CPN and maintaining positive payment history, you can gradually offset the negative marks on your credit report and rebuild your creditworthiness over time.

Protecting Your SSN: One of the primary benefits of using a CPN is its ability to shield your Social Security Number from potential risks, such as identity theft or fraud.

By using a CPN instead of your SSN for credit-related activities, you can minimize the likelihood of unauthorized access to your personal information and mitigate the impact of any fraudulent activity on your credit report.

In my experience, using a CPN to build or repair credit requires a combination of patience, discipline, and vigilance. It's not a quick fix or a guaranteed solution, but rather a tool that, when used responsibly, can help you achieve your financial goals over time.

However, it's crucial to approach the use of CPNs with caution and integrity. While they may offer privacy and security benefits, they're not a loophole or a shortcut to financial success. Using a CPN irresponsibly or engaging in fraudulent activities can have serious consequences, including legal repercussions and further damage to your credit.

CHAPTER 3

Step-by-step guide on how to legally obtain a CPN

Step 1: Research and Education

Before diving into the process of obtaining a CPN, it's crucial to educate yourself about what CPNs are, their purpose, and the legal and ethical considerations surrounding their use. Take the time to research reputable sources, consult with financial experts or legal professionals if needed, and familiarize yourself with the laws and regulations governing CPNs in your jurisdiction.

Step 2: Determine Your Eligibility

CPNs are not available to everyone, and there are specific criteria that must be met to qualify for one. Typically, individuals who are unable to obtain credit using their Social Security Number (SSN) due to identity theft, financial distress, or other extenuating circumstances may be eligible for a CPN. Assess your situation and determine whether applying for a CPN is the right choice for you.

Step 3: Select a Reputable Provider

Once you've determined that you're eligible for a CPN, the next step is to select a reputable provider to assist you in obtaining one. Be wary of companies or individuals promising quick fixes or guaranteed results, as these may be signs of fraudulent activity. Instead, look for providers with a track record of legitimacy, transparency, and customer satisfaction. Research online reviews, ask for recommendations from trusted sources, and verify the credentials of any provider you're considering.

Step 4: Submit Your Application

Once you've chosen a provider, you'll need to submit an application for a CPN. This typically involves providing personal information, such as your name, date of birth, and address, as well as documentation to verify your identity and eligibility. Be prepared to provide copies of documents such as your driver's license, passport, or utility bills, as well as any additional information requested by the provider.

Step 5: Receive Your CPN

After submitting your application, you'll need to wait for your CPN to be issued. The processing time can vary depending on the provider and your individual circumstances, so be patient during this step. Once your CPN has been issued, you'll receive it via email or postal mail, along with any instructions or additional information provided by the provider.

Step 6: Safeguard Your CPN

Once you've received your CPN, it's crucial to safeguard it as you would your Social Security Number. Treat your CPN with the same level of confidentiality and care, and be cautious about sharing it with others. Avoid using your CPN for purposes other than those for which it was intended, and be mindful of the legal and ethical implications of its use.

Step 7: Use Your CPN Responsibly

With your CPN in hand, you can begin using it for credit-related activities such as applying for loans, credit cards, or other financial products. However, it's essential to use your CPN responsibly and ethically, making timely payments, maintaining good financial habits, and adhering to the laws and regulations governing CPN usage. Remember that your CPN is a tool to help you achieve your financial goals, but it's up to you to use it wisely.

In my experience, obtaining a CPN legally and responsibly requires careful consideration, thorough research, and adherence to applicable laws and regulations.

CHAPTER 4

Tips for choosing a reputable CPN provider or service

Do Your Research: Before choosing a CPN provider, it's essential to conduct thorough research. Start by searching online for providers in your area and reading reviews from previous customers. Look for providers with a solid reputation, positive feedback, and a track record of legitimacy and transparency.

Check Credentials and Accreditation: Legitimate CPN providers should have the necessary credentials and accreditation to operate legally. Look for providers that are registered with relevant government agencies or industry associations, and verify their credentials before proceeding.

Avoid Guarantees or Unrealistic Claims: Be wary of CPN providers that make unrealistic promises or guarantees, such as guaranteeing a specific credit score or instant approval for credit. Building or repairing credit takes time and effort, and there are no shortcuts or guarantees when it comes to achieving financial success.

Transparency and Disclosure: Reputable CPN providers should be transparent about their services, fees, and the potential risks and limitations of using a CPN. Look for providers that provide clear and upfront information about their processes, pricing, and terms of service, and avoid those that are evasive or reluctant to answer your questions.

Customer Support and Communication: Choose a CPN provider that offers excellent customer support and communication. Look for providers that are responsive to your inquiries, provide timely updates on the status of your application, and are available to address any concerns or issues that may arise.

Legal Compliance: Ensure that the CPN provider you choose operates in compliance with applicable laws and regulations governing CPN usage. Avoid providers that engage in illegal or unethical practices, such as selling CPNs that are stolen or obtained through fraudulent means.

Referrals and Recommendations: Consider seeking referrals or recommendations from trusted sources, such as friends, family members, or financial advisors who have experience with CPNs. Personal recommendations can provide valuable insights and help you make an informed decision when choosing a CPN provider.

Read the Fine Print: Before signing any agreements or contracts with a CPN provider, carefully read and understand the terms and conditions. Pay close attention to any fees, charges, or obligations associated with the service, and seek clarification on any terms that are unclear or ambiguous.

www.ingramcontent.com/pod-product-compliance
Lightning Source LLC
Chambersburg PA
CBHW071221240526
45470CB00018B/2191